Ferris Wheels,

Daffodils

& Hot Fudge Sundaes

Ferris Wheels,

Daffodils

& Hot Fudge
Sundaes

A Journal of Gratitude

LAURA JENSEN WALKER

Fleming H. Revell
A Division of Baker Book House Co
Grand Rapids, Michigan 49516

© 2002 by Laura Jensen Walker

Published by Fleming H. Revell
a division of Baker Book House Company
P.O. Box 6287, Grand Rapids, MI 49516-6287

Printed in the United States of America

Library of Congress Cataloging-in-Publication Data

Walker, Laura Jensen.
    Ferris wheels, daffodils & hot fudge sundaes : a journal of gratitude / Laura Jensen Walker.
        p.   cm.
    ISBN 0-8007-1797-X
    1. Gratitude. 2. Women—Diaries. I. Title.
BF575.G68 W35 2002
179′.9—dc21   2001048546

For current information about all releases from Baker Book House, visit our web site:
                    http://www.bakerbooks.com

To God, from whom all blessings flow,
with eternal gratitude

And to Michael, the love of my life:
Je t'aime

Introduction

When I wrote *Thanks for the Mammogram!* out of my desire to try to help women—and those who love them—going through breast cancer, I ended the book with a final chapter that included a portion of a "list of thanks." That little list was begun during one of my hospital stays for chemotherapy.

I couldn't believe the outpouring of e-mails, letters, and calls I received in response to the book, and in particular, that last chapter. Wow! Here's just a sampling:

"As I read through your list, each page triggered my own thankful thoughts which I wanted to write down then and there."—L. D.

"I just finished reading *Thanks for the Mammogram!* I couldn't put it down. It really is a book I will long remember. Your list of gratitude was so touching—what a beautiful and simple thing to do."—M. O.

"Your final chapter in the book inspired me to start a journal thanking God for all my blessings. (Your name and book are included.)" —L. P.

"So many things for which you were thankful touched a chord in me." —C. M.

"I really loved your book, especially that last chapter! It really makes you stop and think about the things you're thankful for."—D. P.

"When I saw kindred spirits as one of the things on your 'thankful for' list, I almost cried—my daughter and I have always loved *Anne of Green Gables,* and Anne was always searching for kindred spirits."—D. N.

"I truly appreciated and understood your Thankful List. I've always kept 'gratitude' lists in my journal."
—E. D.

"Reading all the things you were thankful for made me start thinking about what I was grateful for in my own life, so I started my 'list of thanks.' So far, I've come up with 140 things!" —S. H.

Although that partial list (there wasn't enough room to include it all in *Thanks for the Mammogram!*) was initially a result of a momentous event in my life—facing the prospect of death—it has continued to this day, long after that threat has passed.

You don't have to be near death to feel gratitude for life and all its many blessings. Thanksgiving enlarges the heart and soul and draws us nearer to God.

For everything God created is good, and nothing is to be rejected if it is received with thanksgiving.

1 TIMOTHY 4:4

As a result of all the kind comments, and more, I was inspired to "finish" my list—although it will never truly be finished since each day brings new thoughts of gratitude.

You're holding the by-product in your hands—a journal of thanksgiving. I hope you like it.

Inside, you'll find serious things and silly things, childlike things and grown-up things, universal things and pertinent-only-to-me things. As you read through the list, you'll find it may spark specific things for which you too are thankful. Use the blank pages in this book to write them down.

And you might want to keep this journal next to your bed, so that when you wake up in the middle of the night and can't sleep, you can jot down those things for which you're thankful.

That's how it all began for me.

A Journal of Gratitude

that I'm alive
my soul-mate husband
chocolate
Dreyer's cookies-and-cream ice cream
my Bible
chemotherapy that worked
family that always comes through when I need them

no more Brussels sprouts—ever!

seeing *Les Miserables* on Broadway—fifth row from
    the front
quiet evenings at home in front of the fire with
    Gracie at our feet
mammograms
belly laughs
Band-Aids
gentle phlebotomists
Casablanca
Sing along with Mitch!
The Lennon Sisters
band shells in small-town parks
my hearing
tears of joy
barbershop quartets

shooting marbles with my brothers
cold lakes on hot summer days
playing cribbage with my Grandpa Miller
Etch-a-Sketch
pink cotton candy at the fair

*eating the middle
of an Oreo first*

corn dogs and Cracker Jack
Ferris wheels and stopping at the top
Pepto Bismol
show-and-tell
tapioca pudding
friends who listen
forgiveness
benign lumps
going to the top of the Empire State Building—
    even though Cary Grant wasn't there
nephews named Josh who know how to program
    my computer
that first amazing view of the Grand Canyon
thatched roof cottages in the Cotswolds
sight
old *National Geographics*
beloved hymns
my Texas cousins and their charming drawl
the scene in *Chariots of Fire* when Eric Liddell says
    in that great Scottish burr, "I believe that God
    made me for a purpose . . . but he also made me
    fast. And when I run, I feel his pleasure."
Bernadette Peters singing "Being Alive"

One single grateful thought raised to heaven is the most perfect prayer.

G. E. LESSING

As the years pass,
I am coming
more and more
to understand that
it is the common,
everyday blessings
of our common,
everyday lives
for which
we should be
particularly
grateful.

LAURA INGALLS WILDER

A grateful mind, by owing owes not,
But still pays, at once
Indebted and discharged.

JOHN MILTON

_____

_____

_____

_____

_____

_____

_____

_____

_____

_____

_____

_____

_____

_____

_____

_____

_____

_____

_____

_____

_____

_____

my husband singing his wedding vows to me

courtesy

honor

kindly white-haired grandmothers who loved the Lord

singing "They Call the Wind Mariah" on a windy day in the Black Forest hills of Germany and hearing it echo back

fidelity

coming out of anesthesia

Louis Armstrong and Ella Fitzgerald duets

the poetry of Byron, Keats, and Shelley

Piccadilly Circus, Trafalgar Square, and Paddington Station

The National Gallery in London

comfortable shoes

train rides in foreign lands

having hair to brush again

I Remember Mama with Irene Dunne

Puccini in the morning

long, drowsy afternoons at the library

breath

making snow angels

snowball fights

Thanksgiving turkey, mashed potatoes and homemade gravy, baked yams with marshmallows, broccoli casserole, pumpkin pie and whipped cream

leftovers

baking Christmas cookies with my mom and my sister every year

Everywhere and in every way . . . we
acknowledge this with profound gratitude.

ACTS 24:3

making new traditions

The Parent Trap with Hayley Mills

The final scene in *White Christmas* where Bing Crosby and Danny Kaye lead the room in singing to their forgotten general, "We'll follow the old man wherever he wants to go . . ."

a perfect Irish tenor singing "Danny Boy"

real knights in shining armor

Jimmy Carter, Dietrich Bonhoeffer, Alexander Solzhenitsyn

the anticipation of heavenly reunions

summer vacations

backyard barbecues

paper plates

high school marching bands and drill teams

drum and bugle corps

morning devotions

The Salvation Army

Billy Graham crusades

The Miracle on 34th Street

"Attaboy, Clarence"

"Silent Night, Holy Night"

my aunt Sharon

Jeremiah 29:11

my favorite pen pal, Grace

Dusty, my fellow bookworm friend

little Bonnie of the soft dark curls and big gray eyes who melts my heart

seeing Rodin's *The Thinker* outdoors in a Paris park

A joyful and pleasant thing it is
to be thankful.

PRAYER BOOK (1662)

Holland's Keukenhof tulip festival
The Art Institute of Chicago
Wisconsin grandfathers
beloved uncles
Kraft marshmallow fudge
strawberries dipped in chocolate
hot buttermilk biscuits dripping with butter and
    honey
happy childhood hours in the basement watching
    my artist father paint
Albert Schweitzer and his hospital at Lambaréné
old country churches with stained glass windows

sleepovers

church potlucks
Grandma's recipes
cookies and milk at bedtime
butterfly kisses
vacation Bible school
Girl Scout cookies
playground swings, kickball, and my first bicycle
Mary Poppins feeding the birds
learning to play the bass ukulele in sixth grade
Gordon MacRae and Shirley Jones singing "If I
    Loved You"
Betty Hutton doing anything Howard Keel can
    do—only better
Judy Garland's "The Man That Got Away"
sausage-and-cheese pizza and strawberry sodas at
    Durango's Pizza Parlor

*Gratitude is not only the greatest of virtues,
but the parent of all the others.*

CICERO

sipping a Green River at Ronsholdt's drugstore in West Racine

following the magical Yellow Brick Road with Dorothy every year

iced tea in the summertime

microwave popcorn and Friday night videos at home

sisters-in-law who are also dear friends

twin nieces

the warm red bathrobe my husband made me for the cold days of chemo

the five-and-dime

Grandma Adelaide

Placido Domingo

John Denver's "Matthew"

God's opening a window after closing a door

National Velvet with the young, wide-eyed Elizabeth Taylor

fields of lavender

babbling brooks

foreign exchange students

seeing *Evita* in the West End of London

that when "the cords of death entangled me" God freed me with his perfect peace and comfort (Psalm 18)

not having to watch Monday night football ever again!

Peter, Paul, and Mary singing "Puff the Magic Dragon"

Volksmarching outside of Munich

In any prosperity of ourselves or others,
we must not omit to testify our recognition
of God's hand by praise and thanksgiving.

JOHN CALVIN

favorite John Wayne movies: *The Quiet Man,*
The Man Who Shot Liberty Valance, and
The Searchers

mornings

a honeymoon on the Northern California coast

that God is a matchmaker

buttermilk pancakes with warm maple syrup and
a tall, cold glass of milk

The Byron room at Grey Gables Inn in Sutter
Creek

sleep

romantic indoor picnics of fried chicken, cheese
and crackers, and strawberries dipped in sour
cream, then rolled in brown sugar

gracious hospitality

Anne of Green Gables

the "Kids Say the Darndest Things" segment of
The Art Linkletter Show

sweetly sung lullabies

Michael's lasagna

English trifle with Bird's custard

Marie Callender's sour cream lemon pie

Tupperware

living in a 350-year-old pink stone cottage in a
small English village

secret gardens

a child's handmade Christmas gift

Saint Augustine

Robert Browning and Elizabeth Barrett Browning

the Song of Solomon

I thank my God every time I remember you.

my mother's love

my father's dreams

weeping willows

sentimental journeys

Yosemite

Bach, Beethoven, Brahms, and Mozart

Judy Garland singing "Have Yourself a Merry Little Christmas"

checks that don't bounce

the Southern humor of Lewis Grizzard

Campbell's tomato soup and grilled cheese sandwiches

peanut butter and jelly sandwiches with a glass of chocolate milk

refunds from the IRS

Candyland

faith, hope, and charity

Wycliffe Bible Translators

"whither thou goest, I will go . . ."

flights of fancy

old cemeteries

God's perfect timing

warm, baggy sweaters

Charles Dickens

Ben Franklin

Chutes and Ladders

reading Luke 2 on Christmas morning

that first snowfall of winter

It is another's fault if he be ungrateful,
but it is mine if I do not give.
To find one thankful man, I will oblige
a great many that are not so.

SENECA

singing duets with my sister in our great-
   grandma's living room
kindness, gentleness, and compassion
The Mary Tyler Moore Show
comfort foods: open-faced hot turkey sandwiches,
   pot roast, applesauce
banana pudding with Nilla Wafers
yellow school buses
swaying with my sweetie to Sinatra
Lena Horne singing "Stormy Weather"

reading in bed

primroses in January
Jan Karon's Mitford books
reruns of *The Dick Van Dyke Show*
meeting Michael at a singles retreat
   in the mountains
going to a couples retreat with Michael
that God said, "It is not good for the man to be
   alone. I will make a helper suitable for him."
   —Genesis 2:18
leaving the hospital oncology ward
eating ice-cream cones while window-shopping
   with my husband when all the stores are closed
"Scarlet Ribbons"
God's faithfulness
shared confidences
ice skating
Tennyson's *Crossing the Bar*
Ivanhoe

. . . but sweeter yet
the still small voice of gratitude.

THOMAS GRAY

"the best of times . . . the worst of times . . ."

Dion's "Abraham, Martin and John"

huddled together as a family around the TV set
watching Neil Armstrong take that "one small
step" on the moon

church Christmas pageants

Good Friday and the Via Dolorosa

"The Old Rugged Cross"

my Scandinavian heritage

thinking on whatever is noble, pure, and lovely

homemade chocolate chip cookies fresh from the oven

beauty that makes me weep

Colm Wilkinson singing "Bring Him Home"

seeing a bald eagle fly overhead

men and women of integrity

Martin Luther

Abraham Lincoln

Elizabeth the First

the fresh scent of pines

ladybugs

mosquito hawks

citronella candles

the first bulb of spring poking up through the dirt

Blue Willow

rose-patterned English china

Cadbury cream eggs in my Easter basket each year

Don Quixote and his Dulcinea

Richard Kiley singing "The Impossible Dream"

O Lord that lends me life,
Lend me a heart replete with thankfulness.

WILLIAM SHAKESPEARE

promises kept

that God's ways are not our ways

David's heart for God

Carol Lawrence and Larry Kert singing "Tonight"
   in the balcony scene from *West Side Story*

good therapists

the funny pages

freshly polished furniture with that wonderful
   lemon-and-beeswax smell

the cross

"Jesus Loves Me, This I Know"

that my friend Steve said to Michael: "You *have* to
   meet my friend Laura!"

our friends Tom and Sharon singing "All I Ask of
   You" (*Phantom of the Opera*) from the church
   balcony at our wedding

Danish layer cake and Napoleon kringle from
   Racine, Wisconsin

the view of Chicago from the top of the John Han-
   cock Building

New York, New York

walking through Times Square at night

seeing the Statue of Liberty through the pay tele-
   scope on the Empire State Building

Rockefeller Center

the best—and biggest—cheesecake in the world at
   the Carnegie Deli

rejection slips that keep me persevering

my first book tour

God is glorified, not by our groans,
but by our thanksgivings.

EDWIN PERCY WHIPPLE

the stretch limo ride from Yonkers to Connecticut
taxi drivers who know where they're going
Atlanta's Southern hospitality
seeing the houses of my youth again
visiting my sixth grade teacher's class and show-
ing her students that dreams do come true
watching Fourth of July fireworks from the shore
of Lake Michigan as a child

*kisses from
my beloved*

the music of Glenn Miller
peanut butter and banana sandwiches
the Sequoias
Rosemary Clooney singing Duke Ellington or
Cole Porter
Sandi Patty singing "The Star Spangled Banner"
Amy Grant singing "El Shaddai"
family reunions with Wisconsin relatives I hadn't
seen in thirty years
weekly Bible studies
accountability
celluloid heroes
Henry Fonda as *Mister Roberts*
Gary Cooper in *Sergeant York* and *Pride of the
Yankees*
Emma Thompson in *Sense and Sensibility*
Leonardo da Vinci and Michelangelo
the light in a Turner painting
Wordsworth's *Tintern Abbey*
hummingbirds in the backyard

*Sometimes our light goes out but is blown
into flame by another human being.
Each of us owes deepest thanks to those
who have rekindled this light.*

ALBERT SCHWEITZER

Mapblast for the directionally impaired (moi)
eyebrow pencil to sketch in those missing chemo
    brows
Visine
mousse—the edible chocolate kind as well as the
    stuff for my hair
Cry, the Beloved Country
"Blessed Assurance"
The 2nd Chapter of Acts' *Hymns* tape

Romans 8:28
Ephesians, Philippians, and Colossians
Catherine Marshall
Debbie Reynolds as *The Singing Nun*
the Mount Hermon writer's conference
that God made men and women different
Bogie and Bacall in *To Have and Have Not*
Bogie and Hepburn in *The African Queen*
Spencer's Mountain and *The Waltons*
my husband and his childlike delight in Christ-
    mas and Disneyland
Chuck Swindoll and Chuck Smith
Shirley Temple and Bill "Bojangles" Robinson tap-
    dancing together
making it through trials together
Carol Burnett, dressed in drapes—curtain rod and
    all—in that hilarious *Gone with the Wind* sketch
    with Harvey Korman playing the Rhett Butler
    role
those Cartwright boys from the Ponderosa

*Sing and make music in your heart
to the Lord, always giving thanks
to God the Father for everything.*

EPHESIANS 5:19–20

Jarrod, Nick, and Heath from *The Big Valley*
split pea soup with ham
hot apple cider with cloves and cinnamon sticks
simmering potpourri
New England in the fall
my uncle's hand-me-down Navy pea coat
the infectious giggle of a child
finding a favorite Trixie Belden mystery from
    childhood in an antique store
the first view of my hometown from the air after
    I've been away far too long

*that he says padittle
and I say perditto:
(kissing my sweetie
when we spot a car
with only one
headlight)*

Beeman's chewing gum
homemade beeswax candles with pressed
    wildflowers
the hoot of an owl
The Red Skelton Show
Andy Williams Christmas specials
not receiving a Christmas fruitcake
double coupon day at the grocery store
that other people are good at math (someone has
    to be)
claw-foot bathtubs
meeting deadlines

Only when we are no longer afraid
do we begin to live in every experience,
painful or joyous, to live in gratitude
for every moment, to live abundantly.

DOROTHY THOMPSON

_____

_____

_____

_____

_____

_____

_____

_____

_____

_____

_____

_____

_____

_____

_____

_____

_____

_____

_____

_____

celebrating *after* the deadline

Judy Garland and Barbra Streisand singing their duet on Judy's TV show

my health

Paul Stookey's "The Wedding Song"

my husband singing "I Will Be Here"

quiet contemplation

not needing to use Spellcheck

buying our first piece of furniture together—an old Singer treadle sewing machine

relaxing in a tub of Radox bath salts and feeling the stress of the day disappear

the jumbo box of crayons with the built-in sharpener at the back

*laughing so hard,
tears roll down my
cheeks*

the salad bar at Sizzler

black lab puppies

the off switch on the telephone ringer

hitting the mute button on the remote during commercials

thick terry cloth towels warm from the dryer

crisp, cool sheets against bare skin

flannel sheets on cold winter nights

Neapolitan ice cream for those times when I can't decide between chocolate, vanilla, or strawberry

fresh squeezed lemonade on a hot summer day

first dibs on the bathroom after a long drive in the country

*Gratitude is a fruit of great cultivation;
you do not find it among gross people.*

SAMUEL JOHNSON

an organized filing system
The 1812 Overture
Gershwin's *Rhapsody in Blue*
Porgy and Bess
wandering through fragrant rose gardens
yellow marshmallow Peeps at Easter
that final chemo treatment three weeks before
    Christmas
Academy Award parties
playing Silver Screen Trivial Pursuit with other
    movie buffs
Charades, Scrabble, and Monopoly
Dixieland jazz

permanent press

The Bobbsey Twins
seeing Seurat's *A Sunday Afternoon on the Island of
    La Grande Jatte* in Chicago
paid-off credit cards
when "customer service" meant something
lazing in a hammock on a slow summer afternoon
A Tree Grows in Brooklyn—book and movie
Cheaper by the Dozen—ditto
daydreaming
cherished record albums
Carole King's *Tapestry* (arguably the greatest pop
    album ever)
Simon and Garfunkel's *Greatest Hits* (arguably the
    other greatest)
Neil Diamond's *Hot August Nights* ("Are you still
    there, tree people?")

Then he took the seven loaves and the fish,
and when he had given thanks, he broke them
and gave them to the disciples,
and they in turn to the people.

MATTHEW 15:36

good credit

owning our own home for the first time after years of renting

Judy Collins sending in the clowns

that 1974 trip to Las Vegas and the thrill of seeing Liza Minnelli Live! (after many, many months of pretending to be her in my living room)

room service

freshly painted living rooms in butter yellow with bright white crown moulding

my dad's painting hung over the fireplace

Barbra Streisand's voice

Fred Astaire's feet

seeing John Denver in concert—twice

freshly mown grass

Cluny Brown

the opportunity to see my "aunt" Annette for the first time in years—just two weeks before she died

stuffed mushrooms and crusty garlic bread

steak and lobster specials

shiny yellow rain slickers

Amish quilts

the babe in the manger

little drummer boys

decorating the Christmas tree

"The First Noel"

Fattigmans bakkels (Norwegian Christmas cookies dusted with powdered sugar)

To speak gratitude is courteous and pleasant,
to enact gratitude is generous and noble,
but to live gratitude is to touch heaven.

JOHANNES A. GAERTNER

---

watching the original version of *How the Grinch Stole Christmas* every year

tobogganing

warm blankets and hot chocolate with mini marshmallows

Peppy, my cousins' dog, saving me by pulling me from the frozen pond after the ice broke when I was seven

Norman Rockwell and *The Saturday Evening Post*

gentle dentistry

Gregory Peck as Atticus Finch in *To Kill a Mockingbird*

working in my pajamas

back rubs after a long day of being hunched over the computer

looking out the kitchen window as I wash the dishes

successful book signings

hour-long phone calls with best friends

getting rid of call waiting

being able to type 100 words a minute

sticky notes

the year Michael planted me a bed of daffodils as a Valentine's surprise

regaining my energy

feeding the ducks and swans at the pond

watching the Macy's parade on TV at Thanksgiving

E. T. pointing to his heart as he says good-bye to Elliott: "I'll be right here."

Beethoven's "Für Elise"

Mickey Mouse suspenders under Michael's tux on our wedding day

Remember that not to be happy
is not to be grateful.

ELIZABETH CARTER

falling asleep with my husband in the spoons
    position
linen tablecloths and cloth napkins
books of quotations
blowing bubbles in my milk when I was a kid
banana cream pie
cashews
dental floss
squeezing into a skinny drugstore photo booth with
    my best friend to get four pictures for fifty cents

splashing
in puddles

sincere thanks
letters from readers
sisters who love to read
that same sister going back to college in her forties
knowing that I'll see my father again someday
peppermint stick ice cream
turning cartwheels in the park
spontaneity
rolling down a grassy hill as an adult
old oak church pews worn smooth by time
the sun filtering through stained glass windows
meditating on God's Word
the first robin of spring
the musicals of Stephen Sondheim
The Tonight Show with Johnny Carson
Natalie Cole singing the "Unforgettable" duet
    "with" her dad, Nat King Cole
nylons that don't bag at the knees

My whole heart rises up to bless
Your name in pride and thankfulness.

ROBERT BROWNING

cars that don't break down
caring oncology nurses
lighthouses
sunrise over the lake
a quiet walk under the full moon
the Big Dipper
being able to identify Orion in the night sky
hearing the whale's tail slap the water while whale
    watching in Monterey
swing sets, merry-go-rounds, and teeter-totters
a kind shoulder to cry on
friends who love me in spite of myself
no more blind dates

giggling

playing board games with my husband
driving across the Golden Gate Bridge
the Santa Cruz boardwalk
August 4th
bake sales
talent shows
craft fairs
Bambi and his friends Thumper and Flower
someone else to put the worm on the fishhook
mission trips to Mexico
volunteering at an orphanage
singing Christmas carols at nursing homes
people who stand up for their faith or right
    "unrightable" wrongs
wishing on a shooting star

My cheeks have often been bedew'd
With tears of thoughtful gratitude.

ROBERT SOUTHEY

knowing I'm not alone

terms of endearment (our private pet names for each other . . . not the movie)

Michael's hands on my waist

that weekend in Catalina

hearing my husband say, "I love this [mastectomy] scar because it means I'm going to have you with me for a long time"

talking baby talk with our canine "daughter"

being matron of honor at my best friend's wedding

the sound track from *When Harry Met Sally* featuring Harry Connick Jr.

prawns at the Gilroy Garlic festival

the Wittlich pigfest

our annual spring trip to Daffodil Hill

laughing so hard you start snorting

turning forty

six-year-old puppies with wet noses

Fred Astaire dancing on the ceiling in *Royal Wedding*

ten years of marriage

having cleavage again

Eydie Gorme singing "Fly Me to the Moon"

seeing Steve and Eydie at Caesar's Palace

dusting on Saturdays to the music of Mantovani as a child

singing "Waltzing Matilda" and "Kookaburra Sits in the Old Gum Tree" in grade school

The Red Badge of Courage

square dancing in gym class

Shakespeare in the park

I do thank God for my books
with every fiber of my being.

OSWALD CHAMBERS

my cuckoo clock from Germany's Black Forest

learning the names of flowers: sweet William, bachelor's buttons, Martha Washington geraniums . . .

Songs from a Secret Garden CD

gas masks (see chapter 11 of *Love Handles for the Romantically Impaired*)

New Year's Eve parties for two

setting our goals for the coming year

second dates

Michael's introducing me to the *Les Miz* sound track on our first drive to the ocean

Martin Luther King's *I Have a Dream* speech

a new day

girl talk

favorite books from childhood: *Freckles, Beautiful Joe, My Friend Flicka, Caddie Woodlawn, Johnny Tremain, Hans Brinker and the Silver Skates, The Yearling* . . .

Disney's *Snow White and the Seven Dwarfs*

the *Little House* books

babysitters who let us stay up late

those '60s beach movies with Frankie and Annette

the Donna Reed episode when Shelley Fabares sang "Johnny Angel"

singing "Johnny Angel" karaoke and pretending I'm a teenager in the '50s

chubby-cheeked toddlers

serving my country in the Armed Forces

listening to stories from WAC's and WAF's who served in World War II

Partners in faith, and brothers in distress,
Free to pour forth their common thankfulness.

WILLIAM WORDSWORTH

the USO
Jane Eyre
Oliver Twist
John Gunther's *Death Be Not Proud*
the annual Komen Race for the Cure
seeing my book in a bookstore for the very first
    time
my eye for decorating
oversized Winnie-the-Pooh slippers
having eyelashes again to put mascara on
encyclopedias
literary journalists: John McPhee, Tracy Kidder,
    Tom Wolfe

praying together

Pepsi, not Coke
haircolor to cover the gray
that Michael sews and I don't have to
grape popsicles
hearing the music of the neighborhood ice-cream
    truck
buying a fudgsicle from that same rainbow-colored
    truck
Rosalind Russell's *Auntie Mame*
the snappy dialogue in *His Girl Friday*
Gene Kelly dancing with Cyd Charisse in the
    Singin' in the Rain dream sequence
that ski lesson in the Alps
free military hops (plane flights)
Joan Baez's amazing grace

We thank Thee for this place in which we dwell;
for the love that unites us; for the peace
accorded us this day; for the hope with which
we expect the morrow; for the health,
the work, the food, and the bright skies
that make our lives delightful.

ROBERT LOUIS STEVENSON

visiting Anne Hathaway's cottage in Stratford-upon-Avon

Rosamunde Pilcher's *Coming Home* and *The Shell Seekers*

Maeve Binchy

Agatha Christie and all those delicious Miss Marple and Hercule Poirot mysteries

creativity

the violin

tenor saxophones

Kenny G

drinking hot chocolate in a sidewalk café on the Champs d'Elysees

making the seventeen-mile drive from Monterey to Carmel

not having to do fractions anymore

gliding beneath the Bridge of Sighs in a gondola in Venice

eating moussaka in the Plaka in Athens

the hot water bottle nestled under the covers at the B&B in Edinburgh

Don't Cry for Me Argentina

Elaine Paige singing "Memory"

Anne Lamott taking it bird by bird

finishing my last midterm

kindred spirit editors

mousetraps

Old Glory

Reach to Recovery volunteers

Gratitude is the sign of noble souls.

Aesop

spitting out prunes at church camp when no one was looking

camp counselors

wearing white go-go boots in the fifth grade

Nestle's crunch bars

Entenmann's Heath-bar cookies

Flavia cards

photographs and memories

the first time I made breakfast for my dad on Father's Day and he ate every bite—surreptitiously removing and hiding the big piece of eggshell

walking across a suspension bridge in Northern Wales

reading Little Women and pretending to be Jo

journals that help me remember long-forgotten details

the kind thank-you note that said, "Now I'm not afraid of the treatment"

The Urbana Missions Conference

camping out in the backyard

old friends

new friends

Mary and Charlie and that city by the bay

The American Cancer Society's *Making Strides Against Breast Cancer* walkathon

The Best of Bread

Archie comics

Alvin and the Chipmunks singing the Christmas cheer song

Give thanks to the God of gods.

PSALM 136:2

Connie Francis wondering where the boys are

my pretending to be Connie Francis singing "Where the Boys Are"

Bach's *Concerto for Two Violins*

three kinds of popcorn—caramel, cheese, and regular—in large Christmas tins

getting chocolate ice-cream cones with jimmies on top from D.J.'s Ice Cream Parlour

seeing the memorial to the Sullivan Brothers as a child

going to church

Alec Guinness in *The Bridge on the River Kwai* and as Obi-Wan

William Holden's *Picnic*

getting to lick the spoon

Jack Lemmon in *Some Like It Hot*

knowing what Rosebud was

Raisinettes

Toblerone bars

the jumbo movie-pack of Reese's Peanut Butter Cups

Dan Fogelberg singing "Leader of the Band"

Barry Manilow—yes, Barry Manilow!—writing the songs to make the whole world sing

bookstores with high wing-backed chairs for reading

magnolia trees

grape hyacinths

bearded irises

our backyard in the spring

No duty is more urgent than
that of returning thanks.

SAINT AMBROSE

women's book clubs
scholarships to college
professors who encouraged my writing
Old Yeller
Lassie and Timmy on TV
our dog Gracie playing the piano
the Sears Roebuck catalog
apple blossoms
cherry blossoms
my neighbor's camellia bush that hangs over into
   our yard

*growing up
in a small town*

electric lawnmowers
crossing off projects on my to-do list
a commute that goes against the flow of traffic
bottled water
Richard Burton singing *Camelot*
long-anticipated vacations
English pub lunches with double Gloucester
   cheese
Shepherd's pie and Cornish pasties
that we don't have to shovel snow in Sacramento
wind chimes outside the back door
Victorian gazebos and potting sheds
my husband's green thumb
recycling
Vernal Falls
Belgian chocolate
Natalie Wood's Maria in *West Side Story*

[Give] thanks to the Father,
who has qualified us to be partakers of the
inheritance of the saints in the light.

COLOSSIANS 1:12 (NKJV)

the White Cliffs of Dover
taking the ferry from Dover to Calais
Angela's Ashes
the beginning of a beautiful friendship
sunbathing on Sardinia
plenty of sunscreen
floppy straw hats
nobody but Mandy Patinkin singing "High Flying, Adored"
my great-aunt Dorothy and uncle Bill who always kept an open room in their cozy attic for visiting missionaries
the attic that hid Anne Frank and her family
hearing Big Ben chime
84 Charing Cross Road
faded chintz in a country cottage
beveled mirrors and leaded glass windows
comfy overstuffed armchairs

playing hide-and-seek and kick-the-can in the street as a kid

padded window seats just right for reading
Arsenic and Old Lace
The Boxcar Children
The Borrowers
second-grade teachers who read aloud
"For better or worse, for richer or poorer . . ."
female OB-GYN's
Midol
laundromats
rolls of quarters

*I awoke this morning with devout
thanksgiving for my friends, the old and new.*

RALPH WALDO EMERSON

our own washer and dryer

having the energy to do my own laundry again

"Ebbtide"

the first barbecue of summer

roommates who became friends

being able to cook again without getting nauseous

taking a film class in college and getting credit for watching movies

double-stuffed Oreos and milk

pink rubber erasers

Elmer's school paste with the orange applicator

learning how to do papier-mâche and decoupage
   in the sixth grade

spelling bees

seventh-grade gymnastics

walking to school

wearing long pants to elementary school under
   my skirt on blustery days

best friends who helped me take a bath after
   surgery

tenderness

courage

twenty-five-year friendships

endurance

the Delany sisters' *Having Our Say*

Let the peace of Christ rule in your hearts,
since as members of one body you were called
to peace. And be thankful.

COLOSSIANS 3:15

the friend who pitches in without having
   to be asked
visiting the Tower of London and keeping my
   head
the friend who's always willing to read my first
   drafts (Thanks, Katie!)
stopping by Muir Woods on a sunny day
being married to my best friend
morning glories, snapdragons, and lily-of-the-valley
lilacs and forget-me-nots
the *Sunset Western Garden Book*
Paul Scofield as *A Man for All Seasons*

*someone else
to mow the lawn*

"It Is Well with My Soul"
Mother Teresa's example
Japanese maples
wheelbarrows
Big Band music
boating as a child with my uncle Bob and aunt
   Lorraine
attempting to water-ski
the scenic drive up to Lake Tahoe
thrift store shopping in New York's Greenwich
   Village
bagfuls of Tsatsuma mandarin oranges
Pippin apples
the Garden of Eden
Doris Day's secret love
dinner at The Old Milano Hotel in Gualala
The Prayer of Jabez

I am glad that he thanks God for anything.

SAMUEL JOHNSON

Good Samaritans
considerate neighbors
Welcome Wagons
Erma Bombeck
freesia, jonquils, and ranunculus
crepe myrtles in bloom
old Broadway favorites
Ethel Merman's "There's No Business Like Show Business"
Julie Andrews dancing all night
Rex Harrison growing accustomed to her face
honeymoon showers built for two
Saturday morning farmer's markets

finished sprinkler systems

visiting some of Hemingway's haunts in Paris
Mark Spitz and his seven gold medals
Peggy Fleming
having a choice between saline or silicone
Snickers candy bars
Crock-Pots™ and pressure cookers
well-stocked medicine cabinets
the sweetness of Down's syndrome children
my friend Lana's Special Ed class
Princess Diana's heart
Audrey Hepburn's grace and compassion
the last picture my dad ever painted: a portrait of my grandpa
kindergarten
open hearts

A proud man is seldom a grateful man, for he never thinks he gets as much as he deserves.

HENRY WARD BEECHER

happy endings
stopping at roadside fruit and vegetable stands
Slinkies and yo-yos
hot dog stands and frosty root beer floats
sticky warm cinnamon rolls fresh from the oven
digging my toes in the sand at the beach
finding a perfect sand dollar
secrets shared
God's providence

kind oncologists

egg rolls
chicken chow mein
ultrasounds that come out okay
Andrea Macardle knowing everything will be okay
    tomorrow
Pippin looking for his corner of the sky
the cast of *Les Miz* singing "One Day More"
the Trinity
English ivy
fields of bluebells
mixed bouquets
every song in *The Secret Garden*
running through sprinklers on a hot day
moving away from the Arizona heat
mints on the pillow, thick terry cloth robes, and
    all the other pampering that comes with staying
    in a high-class hotel
London bobbies who don't carry guns
rolling pins and cookie cutters
whistling teakettles

Gratitude is not only the memory
but the homage of the heart rendered
to God for his goodness.

NATHANIEL P. WILLIS

_____

_____

_____

_____

_____

_____

_____

_____

_____

_____

_____

_____

_____

_____

_____

_____

_____

_____

_____

_____

_____

_____

_____

_____

PG Tips tea

an encouraging word

speakers bureaus

making it through Air Force tech school in four
  weeks instead of ten

procrastinating the not-that-important task in
  favor of a much-needed nap

Pride and Prejudice, Emma, and *Persuasion*

that I don't live in the days of *Tess of the
  D'Urbervilles*

*a second
bathroom*

the BBC

public television

National Public Radio and Garrison Keillor

singing in the cherub choir at the Lutheran Holy
  Communion Church of my childhood

kickball

hopscotch

jumping rope in the street in front of our house

playing statuemaker in the wintertime

making snow forts at my grandma's house

well-stocked pantries

the Farmer in the Dell

my old Chatty Cathy doll

playing Mystery Date with my girlfriends

Dolly Parton's rendition of her song "I Will
  Always Love You"

Botticelli's *Venus*

California's missions

When the heart overflows with gratitude . . .

WALTER SAVAGE LANDOR

the healing power of laughter
Tom Sawyer and *The Adventures of Huckleberry Finn*
Uncle Tom's Cabin
small boxes of raisins
the color cobalt blue
delftware
blue-and-white Staffordshire china
crackle logs

someone else to clear out the rubbish

privacy
Meryl Streep
that Tuesday afternoon at the de Young Museum
calendars and Daytimers
Russian writers
"La Vie en Rose"
music boxes that play "Lara's Theme"
making up stories for my nieces and nephews
travel videos
disco dancing in Europe in the '70s
Bette Midler singing the theme from *Beaches* ("Wind Beneath My Wings")
the family photo gallery in our hallway
clear bone scans
Sarah Brightman and Andrea Bocelli singing "Time to Say Goodbye"
bright red zinnias and double begonias
a bouquet of daisies
when the neighbors are quiet

The essence of all beautiful art,
all great art, is gratitude.

FRIEDRICH NIETZSCHE

a PICC line (my portable catheter IV) so I
    wouldn't get poked anymore
favorite romantic movies: *It Happened One Night,
    Gone with the Wind, An Affair to Remember,
    Bringing Up Baby, The Philadelphia Story* . . .
The Princess Bride and "twoo wuv"
Harrison Ford raiding the lost ark
simple silver wedding bands

leaving the emergency room

the double wedding ring quilt wall hanging
    Michael made for me
garage sale-ing on Saturday mornings with my
    honey
the peddler's faire in Old Town Folsom
my fountain pen going-away gift
stargazing in the mountains far away from city
    lights
topiaries and raised flower beds
plate hangers—without them, my kitchen walls
    would be bare
the first overwhelming sight of *Winged Victory* in
    the Louvre
eating pizza at the very first Shakey's
The Irish Tenors singing "I'll Take You Home
    Again, Kathleen"
Impressionism
the roomful of Degas at The Metropolitan
    Museum of Art
that Mary Cassatt didn't listen to her father and
    painted anyway

Let us be grateful to people who make us happy—they are the charming gardeners who make our souls blossom.

MARCEL PROUST

Renoir's *Two Sisters* and *Woman at the Piano*
Mary Engelbreit cards
Hallmark stores
the Special Olympics
poet friends
that I like my in-laws
Toastmasters
a branch of dogwood
Proverbs 19:11
the medication that brought my blood count back
    to normal
Chopin
tour guides
Sister Wendy explaining the world's greatest
    paintings in her wonderful accent

built-in dishwashers

our annual June visit to the local art festival
the opening of *Oklahoma!* with Gordon MacRae's
    lush singing in the cornfield
refrigerator art
favorite English mystery authors: Anne Perry, P. D.
    James, Elizabeth George
Daphne du Maurier's *Rebecca* and *My Cousin Rachel*
books in every room
Alfred Hitchcock movies
Stephen King's *On Writing*
Roget's Super Thesaurus
my husband's homemade carrot cake
the Rodin collection at San Francisco's Palace of
    the Legion of Honor

Give thanks to the LORD, call on his name.

1 CHRONICLES 16:8a

Camille Claudel's sculptures

Vivaldi's *Four Seasons*

thermostats

weekday matinees when the movie theater's
almost empty

the heady scent of star jasmine

when the stitches are removed

the theme from *Somewhere in Time*

C. S. Lewis

Bonhoeffer's *The Cost of Discipleship*

the Sunday paper

reading aloud to my husband at night

air-conditioning

B&B cookbooks

all-in-one measuring spoons

salt, sugar, flour, eggs, and vanilla

frosting-in-a-can

microwaves

the "Be Our Guest" production number from Disney's *Beauty and the Beast*

scones

beamed ceilings and built-in bookcases

Anthony Hopkins

passion

holding hands while we walk Gracie around the
block

the Galt Flea Market on Tuesdays

hollyhocks and delphiniums in front of a white
picket fence

*If you haven't all the things you want,
be grateful for the things you don't have
that you wouldn't want.*

ANONYMOUS

Jimmy Stewart's *Rear Window*

stir-frying in a wok

when the quiche turns out perfect

my mom's homemade brownies

Ephesians 5:31: "For this reason a man will leave his father and mother . . ."

sponge baths

friends who live on the Southern coast of England

Christopher Timothy's audio books of James Herriot stories

that I lived in Europe for five years

Monet's painting of the woman in the field with an umbrella

Steve McQueen's great escape

favorite Sunday school teachers

posing for a sidewalk artist in Montmartre

community theater

my husband in *You Can't Take It with You*

The Love Poems of John Donne

The Antiques Roadshow

soda crackers

Extra-strength Tylenol

emesis basins—and that I don't need them anymore

A Room with a View

airplanes with extra leg room in coach

those fearless tomboy days of childhood

Cat Stevens' "Father and Son"

Max & Marjorie: The Correspondence Between Maxwell E. Perkins & Marjorie Kinnan Rawlings

Enter into His gates with thanksgiving,
And into His courts with praise.
Be thankful to Him, and bless His name.

PSALM 100:4 (NKJV)

live people on the other end of the phone instead of a recorded menu of options
Communion
the unity candle at our wedding
Scott Wesley Brown's "This Is the Day"
that a cord of three strands is not easily broken
wedding photos
my husband making sure I got the necessary pain medications when I was hospitalized
chicken bouillon when I was nauseous
Sean Connery

leaving the appointment with the tax man

fresh starts
a room of my own
Q-tips
cough syrup
handy tissues
"The Lord's Prayer"
"Great Is Thy Faithfulness"
Wind Point lighthouse
working at home
a raft of reference books right at my fingertips
those two-for-one coupon books that elementary kids sell
The Best Years of Our Lives
Mrs. Miniver
Random Harvest
English fish-and-chips shops
window-shopping at Harrod's

If the only prayer you say in your entire life is "thank you" that will suffice.

MEISTER ECKHART

the *Norton Anthology of English Literature*

successful bypass surgeries for cherished aunts and uncles

the back cover of *Reader's Digest*

audio books to listen to in the car

the look on my husband's face when he opened his Christmas present—a life-size framed and matted print of his favorite Monet

Neil Simon's comedies

Jean Shepherd

A Christmas Story

The Vienna Boys Choir

watching Mary Lou Retton score a perfect 10 on the vault

Sam's Club

long-distance calling cards

planning projects together

shopping in London's open-air Petticoat Lane market

going to a museum with one particular painting in mind and then discovering unexpected treasures

Jennifer Holliday singing "And I Am Telling You I'm Not Going"

Patti LuPone dreaming a dream

Michael Crawford's music of the night

freelance assignments

We, Your people and sheep of Your pasture,
Will give You thanks forever; We will show forth
Your praise to all generations.

PSALM 79:13 (NKJV)

souvenirs that take me back to the days I spent
  in Europe
good exchange rates
musty old bookstores
Home Depot
my "girl" hammer (too small for Michael, just right
  for me)
two-car garages
doggy doors
smoke alarms
Renata Tebaldi singing "La Boheme" (which I first
  heard in the movie *Moonstruck*)

making it through
Air Force
basic training

reconstructive surgery
the complimentary valet parking at my oncologist's
  office
good agents
the way the house smells when we're baking bread
Edith Piaf, "the little sparrow," and France's
  national treasure during World War II
driving down to L.A. to audition for the game
  show Tic-Tac-Dough
SuperCuts
volumizing shampoos
moisturizing lotion

Contentment is not satisfaction.
It is the grateful, faithful, fruitful use
of what we have, little or much.

MALTBIE D. BABCOCK

red blazers

community colleges

paint-by-the-numbers

Gilbert & Sullivan

Danny Kaye as Hans Christian Andersen singing "Thumbelina"

organ donors

Ed Ames singing "I Believe"

Mario Lanza's "Ave Maria"

that God's colors aren't limited to the Crayola eight-pack

Mitzi Gaynor washing that man outta her hair

the Garden of Gethsemane

the Book of Job

the Gospel of Matthew

yellow pansies with purple faces

when the calla lilies are in bloom

Tuesdays with Morrie

finally realizing during the eighth month of our marriage that Michael was adding one rose for each anniversary month we'd been wed (it was a math thing)

worshipping God with joyful abandon

my husband singing next to me in church on Sunday mornings

*At whatever straws we must grasp,
there is always a time for gratitude
and new beginnings.*

J. ROBERT MOSKIN

"But the fruit of the Spirit is love, joy, peace, patience, kindness, goodness, faithfulness, gentleness and self-control . . ." (Galatians 5:22–23)

the sight of my first windmill in Holland

solar-powered windmills in California

crepe stands in Paris

the London Underground

the beautiful watercolor quilt wall hanging of the cross made by my Renaissance man

snuggling under the flying geese quilt

anniversary trips to England

getting paid to do what I love!

growing up a tomboy

pedicures—and the chance to read the latest fashion magazines uninterrupted for 45 minutes

reading *Winnie the Pooh*—for the very first time—in my forties

Kenny Loggins and Amy Grant visiting *The House at Pooh Corner*

"girl" days with my best friend

a car with air-conditioning

learning how to type in high school

learning new things

that I enjoy cooking

playing Concentration with my little brother when I babysat him

cobblestone streets

walking across the Yorkshire moors

the heather on the hill

*Any one thing in the creation is sufficient
to demonstrate a Providence
to an humble and grateful mind.*

EPICTETUS

Gene Kelly and Cyd Charisse singing about that
   heather on the hill
Brit Rail passes
visiting Westminster Abbey for the first time
travel guru Rick Steves
coming home

*those times when
we don't watch any
TV for a week*

double-wide filing cabinets
a rolling desk chair
self-adhesive postage stamps (so I don't have to
   lick them anymore)
the breast cancer research postage stamp
bridal showers
the pearl-and-marcasite earrings my mom gave
   me to wear on my wedding day
my grandma's antique white-gold watch that I still
   wear today
being forgiven for saying—or doing—something
   stupid
our spare change jar for England
online writers groups
turned-off cell phones
Billy Elliot
spontaneity
people who don't hold grudges
New England clam chowder in Boston
a big pot of homemade vegetable soup simmering
   on the stove

Thanksgiving is the language of heaven,
and we had better start to learn it
if we are not to be mere dumb aliens there . . .

A. J. GOSSIP

toasted cheese-and-pineapple sandwiches from The Carpenter's Arms in Middle Barton, England

the wonderful aromas that always greeted me when I opened the door to Grandma's house

the days when milkmen still delivered milk to the back door

The Cheapskate Monthly

ATM machines that don't charge fees

miscalculating the amount of an expected royalty check—to my advantage!

everyone who helped me pass my college math class

s'mores

that the fear of the Lord is the beginning of wisdom

the Holy Spirit

books that keep me up to the wee small hours

A Severe Mercy

The Diving Bell and Butterfly

Anne Lamott's *Traveling Mercies*

seeing the statue of George M. Cohan in Times Square

big shady oak trees on hot summer days

the crunch of fall leaves beneath my feet

moments of quiet reflection

plaid skirts and warm, woolly sweaters

white cotton blouses

penny loafers

piggy banks

Love of God is adoration of the only true good;
it is gratitude to the bestower of all gifts; it is
joy in holiness; it is "consent to Being."

H. RICHARD NIEBUHR

my mom's fruit cocktail cake

the black-and-white (house) trail in the
  Cotswolds

discovering the heart-rending music of Eva Cassidy

online shopping

free shipping

my writing friends

cruising down the Rhine River in Germany

partaking of the local culture in foreign lands

working farms

eating shish kebabs and rice just after dusk in a
  backyard dotted with tiki torches and citronella
  candles

*completing a
long-delayed home
improvement*

no mosquitoes

homegrown juicy beefsteak tomatoes

herb gardens

making *Reader's Digest* Christmas trees at my
  grandma's

The Tale of Peter Rabbit

taking a child to his first pumpkin patch

pacifiers

being able to recite favorite lines of movie dialogue with my honey:

> "Randy lay there like a slug. It was his only
>   defense."
> "After all, tomorrow is another day."
> "There's no place like home."

It is only with gratitude
that life becomes rich.

Dietrich Bonhoeffer

my aunt Char who always fixed my hair for elementary school choir concerts

bobby pins, barrettes, and hair scrunchies

grade school assemblies

saying the prayer, "Now I lay me down to sleep . . ." every night with my sister when we were little

people who keep their word

the fresh smell of a summer rain

the parables of Jesus

World Vision, Compassion International, and other child sponsorship charities

my cousin's successful kidney transplant

friends I can depend upon

someone who goes the extra mile

the animal rescue shelter where we found Gracie

that weeping may last for the night, but joy comes in the morning

an unexpected cloudburst

Sarah Brightman's angel of music

the musicals of Andrew Lloyd Webber

antique armoires

home-and-garden magazines

garden statues

white picket fences and rose arbors

Good examples: St. Francis of Assisi, Eric Liddell, Albert Schweitzer, Corrie ten Boom, Billy Graham . . .

Jimmy Carter and Habitat for Humanity

*Prayer is the movement of trust, of gratitude,
of adoration, or of sorrow, that places us
before God, seeing both Him and ourselves
in the light of his infinite truth, and moves us
to ask Him for the mercy, the spiritual
strength, the material help, that we all need.*

THOMAS MERTON

adventurous people who dare to "push the
    envelope"
Charles Lindbergh, Amelia Earhart, Beryl
    Markham
the servicemen and women who fought and
    served in World War II
the men and women who serve their country today
Meg Ryan and Tom Hanks getting mail
Richard Burton and Julie Andrews doing what the
    simple folk do
the cross on a simple silver chain Michael gave me
    for Valentine's Day
Van Morrison's "Brown-Eyed Girl"

dreams that came true

the tracks of Linda Ronstadt's tears
James Taylor's assurance that I've got a friend
friends across the sea
an unexpected income tax return that paid for our
    house to be painted
my subscription to *Romantic Homes* magazine
walking through model homes
knowing where my true home lies
Charlotte Church's "Pie Jesu"
that I know the author of life
the friend who knows just the right thing to say
    or do to lift my spirits
a lift to school
people who practice random acts of kindness
taking the road less traveled

*God has two dwellings: one in heaven,
and the other in a meek and thankful heart.*

IZAAK WALTON

that Beach Boys concert in Cleveland
Krispy Kreme doughnuts
dance recitals
backyard vegetable gardens
summer fruit, freshly picked and eaten while still
  atop the ladder
anonymous generosity
cheerful givers
our pastor with a tender heart

*people who
can tap-dance*

seeing Neil Diamond in concert
free 45's (records) from the pizza parlor jukebox
  where my mom worked
retro coffee shops with tabletop jukeboxes
banana splits from Dairy Queen
pj's with the drop seat bottoms
that first visit to the zoo
Texas barbecues
privacy
Mr. Potato-head
parents who read their children bedtime stories
power naps
a solitary walk along the beach
passing notes in seventh grade
playing by the rules—and knowing when to break
  them
Christmas in July—where we watch all our
  favorite Christmas movies in one day

Gratitude is the most exquisite form of courtesy.

JACQUES MARITAIN

leaving all the doors and windows open to usher
   in the cool summer night breeze
watching the growth of the tree we planted in the
   front yard
praying before a meal—even in public
a grandmother-in-law who rode a Harley-David-
   son in the '20s
the whole new family acquired through marriage
exploring tidal pools and finding glorious living
   sea treasures

*optimists, rather than
pessimists*

fresh flowers in the bathroom
ficus trees that don't die
a big bag of Reese's peanut butter cup miniatures
when a friend recommends—and lends me—a
   wonderful new book to devour
favorite quotes about books and reading:

A book is like a garden carried in the pocket.
   —CHINESE PROVERB

*If the crowns of all the kingdoms of Europe were
laid down at my feet in exchange for my books
and my love of reading, I would spurn them all.*
   —FRANCOIS FÉNELON

*Book love, my friend, is your pass to the greatest,
the purest, and the most perfect pleasure that God
has prepared for his creatures. It lasts when all
other pleasures fade. It will support you when all
other recreations are gone. It will last until your
death. It will make your hours pleasant to you as
long as you live.*
   —ANTHONY TROLLOPE

Gratitude is the heart's memory.

FRENCH PROVERB

parents who instilled in me a love of reading
freshly sharpened pencils
calculators
my happily cluttered home office
the friend who walks a mile in my shoes
home cooking

spontaneous dates with my husband

Aunt Bee, Andy, Opie, Barney, and Goober
my mom's beef stew
our beautiful one-of-a-kind wedding cake made
    by my sister-in-law Debbie
Lucy and Ethel
Mary and Rhoda
Laura and Lana
hearing—and believing—*You'll Never Walk Alone*
    in times of sorrow
seeing my brother Todd live on in his daughter
    Letitia
great-nieces and great-nephews
"There is a friend who sticks closer than a brother"
duets by Mandy Patinkin and Bernadette Peters
Charles Schulz and *Peanuts*
Santa Rosa and midweek trips to Sebastopol
honeysuckle
white gardenias
bright pink azaleas
my friend Pat who led me to the Lord
John 3:16
nine years cancer free

No one is as capable of gratitude as one who has emerged from the kingdom of night.

ELIE WIESEL

*To be grateful is
to recognize the love
of God in everything
He has given us—
and He has given us
everything. Every
breath we draw is a
gift of His love, every
moment of existence
a gift of grace.*

THOMAS MERTON